2υ
THINGS
I WISH I KNEW AT
20

By
Roy Merchant

20 Things I Wish I Knew At 20

First Printed in United Kingdom 2020

Published by Conscious Dreams Publishing
www.consciousdreamspublishing.com

Edited by Elise Abram

ISBN: 978-1-913674-06-9

TO AFUA

The book is sent to you as a gift
for the insight and courage
you have inspired in me
as I watched you from the sidelines.

Vhyen Keent

Dedication

I dedicate this book to my wife, Sue, who watches out for me and over me. Whose love I can feel and whose insights I overlook at my peril.

I also dedicate this book to my children and grandchildren, my precious life's work, who let me know that my masterpiece is almost complete.

I would not ever leave out my brothers, sisters, uncles, aunts, nephews and nieces and all my friends who all collectively make this life of mine so immeasurably pleasurable.

Contents

Preface

This book was initially a section of my autobiography, entitled *Rhythms Of My Life*.

The feedback I received from other writers was that it was too self-contained to be part of another book and should stand alone. I decided to take their advice for a change.

This book has been a labour of love and has taken me a few years to write. As I got into the rewriting and editing, I decided to create a book that was more a reflection on things I could have done better or differently, given hindsight, a bit more wisdom about life, and the pursuit of contentment.

This book describes a wish list of ideas, certainties, philosophies, and beliefs with which I wish I had been armed as I entered my twentieth year of life. In writing this book, I have found out so much about myself and what I love, what works for me, and what my wish list for the planet is, and I am coming to terms with the certainty of life and death.

These 20 things would have helped me to cut through some of the chaos engulfing me as I took my steps into manhood. I hope that, in writing down these thoughts, they may, in some way, help others who may follow me and see the light earlier than I did.

It might also bring a smile – or a knowing kind of smile – to the faces of readers who have travelled the road on which I reflect.

A lot of people have inspired me and given me the will to continue writing, but I would like to give a special thank you to my wife, Sue, who created and maintained an environment in which my thoughts could come through the mist during long, quiet nights in the office. Those quiet moments helped me find the clarity of thought I needed to navigate some of the ideas and questions I had. All the difficulties in having to start again, rewriting, and editing has enabled me to think more deeply about the issues I faced and the solutions I came up with.

I would also like to give thanks to my children, Adrian, Ainsley, and Sophie and my brother, Seymour, who all nodded in the right places when I bored them with my next idea from the "Creative Pool".

The First Thing I Wish I Knew

Uncertainty will Slip into my Certainty

think I was born with a high level of inner-confidence. I have read so much about so many things and aligning that with a reasonably strong memory, a clear sense of world-historical timelines, and a good deductive and logical brain, I could figure a lot of things out, even when I was not sure about them. This ability stood me in good stead as I fought my way onwards and upwards in all aspects of my life.

My recall would bail me out when my logic failed, and my reasoning would rescue me when my ignorance was about to claim victory. This filled me with a high level of self-assurance and certainty. Then came middle age, along with new opportunities and challenges.

As I got older and my courage started to wane, my confidence asked questions I never heard it ask before. It queried everything until I was uncertain about what I was thinking and started asking myself if I was sure.

This was precisely the wrong time in my life for uncertainty to come calling as I was nearing the peak of all that I would achieve in my work life.

My psyche asked questions like what was the purpose of being in government? What was the reason I went flat out to complete my to-do list? What was the beneficial outcome of my efforts to be successful? Did the local community care about any of the issues I was killing myself to resolve? The more I asked these questions, the worse the answers were.

Now, it may have been that my physical and mental energies had reached a saturation point, and I was finding excuses (valid or not) to give up the chase. It could have been wisdom, maturity, or old age knocking on my door, suggesting there was no point in it all, that my task would/could never ever be completed to my satisfaction.

My insight might have been telling me that all careers (large or small) always end in failure, so there was no point in busting the proverbial gut as it got you nowhere. At 20, I wish I knew that this level of cynicism would plague my middle years.

I call it cynicism, but upon reflection, I think it was just the certainty of the size of my task hitting me between the eyes.

If I had known this at 20, I could have planned for it by ignoring the realities a little longer.

The Second Thing I Wish I Knew

I am not Sure about Who I Was or Who I Wanted to be

*I*n the absence of clear and present evidence of who I am and where I was before slavery, I have been cajoled into believing that the best way of showing I existed and proving that I, too, can be successful is to adopt Roman ideals.

The Roman civilization occupied the Mediterranean and most of Europe and North Africa from the time Augustus declared it an empire until the Moors gained ascendancy in the 8th century A.D. Their doctrines and values are still practised in Western society today.

If you have to be – or decide to be – like a modern-day Roman, then be the best Roman you can be. There is no point aiming for less. Do not settle for anything less than second best, as Curtis Mayfield would say.

This raises the question: do we want to be the new Romans, the security guards, resource pool, and supporters of a civilisation that has mistreated us in such appalling manner since 1441, when two Portuguese captains stole 12 people from Cabo Branco – now Mauritania – and took them to Portugal as slaves?

How do we redefine what success should mean to the African diaspora once we escape the clutches of the so-called Western civilisation? Do we just copy and paste what they have shown us to help them perpetuate their story while we remorselessly forget ours and become part of their invisible canvas? Or do we find a new way for humankind to evolve? These are the new questions for the African diaspora to grapple with.

I think that today is the start of tomorrow. As Curtis Mayfield says in *Darker than Blue*:

I know we've come a long, long way...

But let us not be so satisfied for tomorrow can be an even brighter day.

The burning questions now are:

What do we tell our children?

Who are we destined to become?

Will we merely become a new version of the same old brutal, selfish, soulless, uncaring Roman mindset that has plagued Europe from Roman Emperor Augustus through the Catholic kings to the present time? Or are we a newly-evolving human, born from the pain, brutality, savagery, and enough pressure endured over some 400 years to have turned coal into diamonds? I am determined to do something better with the tomorrow I am shaping.

What does success mean? What does it look – or taste – like after the slavery revolution? Or should that be "evolution"?

Had not even considered any of these kind of big issues at 20.

The Third Thing I Wish I Knew

We are Mortal
and Just Passing Through

A t 20, I wish I knew that my energy would not last forever. At that young age, life is an endless list of possibilities, and you do not feel as if you have to worry about anything like the length of your time on Gaia. But it is a race, and try as you might, you will not get everything done before time comes calling, catching you totally unprepared for your next great journey. So, it is best to keep yourself as whole, happy, healthy, and as far from obsessed as life will allow. Relax and play with your friends and smile as much as you can. Share your energy with others, and in time, they will share theirs with you. Most importantly, be at peace with yourself, and you will end up being at peace with others.

I wish I knew then that you must try to live out all of your dreams, rather than think the habits and customs indoctrinated into you by your parents are the right templates for a successful life. You only have one lifetime, and the time frame for it is about 60-70 useful years, if you get there. After that, you are pretty much finished. You say you are alive, you convince yourself that it is all about mind over matter, but really, it is not. If you are still physically fit, your mind has lost all the courage and "try first, worry later" mentality that has driven it for the last 60 years, and what you have left are the uncertainties.

You cannot achieve great things with uncertainty. To meet someone who is in his seventies who looks back to realise that he has helped to fulfil everyone else's dreams while his are still unborn, lifeless, and impatiently waiting in the Must-Get-Around-to-this-One-Day file that has been gathering dust for decades upon decades would be the saddest thing to me. The same could be said for looking back at the things you have achieved in your time – because we all have them – to find that they all have someone else's name on them.

People run around, shouting and bragging about the things they have done single-handedly, but when you look at them, they have your joint signature all over them. Help as many people as you can, but always remember to incorporate your dreams into everything you do. Always be on the lookout for opportunities to fulfil your dreams. Remember that those dreams are tomorrow's realities.

By 20, if only I had worked out that it is the affiliations you discover, nurture, protect, and maintain that repay you in the later years. It is everyone for themselves, and you cannot rely on anyone to ensure that your relationships are safe while you are occupied. Never take it for granted that they are meaningfully defended in your absence. You must find ways of ensuring that you maintain your emotional connections – be it through conversations, laughs, jokes, or whatever else it takes to keep them in bloom. Otherwise, you will get to a certain point and realise that your connections have withered on the vine. This is no one's fault – it is just how it is. We humans are selfish beings.

Do not allow your mind to fill with regret, self-pity, or sad memories of what could/should have been. Revise what could have been into what is possible, and do it now. Save the day. Remember that if you are the NOW, your children will be the TOMORROW.

I wish I could have seen that it is crucial to take love seriously. This is the only thing that makes sense. If you cannot find a God, if you think spirits are only what you drink on a Saturday night or that the mind is a storehouse for your memories and nothing else matters, then love will become the most significant philosophical entity able to change how you feel about things. Without love and faith, there is no hope.

Without hope, there is no point in getting out of bed in the morning because there is no incentive to get up, go out, and change the world. And we exist to change the world. So, find love. Do not give up on it as it will never give up on you. Sometimes, it is in the shade, waiting for you to discover it. Other times, it may be by a brook, waiting for you to turn up so it can make the connection and move on to its next client. Remember that love is a positive, spiritual force in the universe, and although it has to fight a host of negative energies, its ultimate victory is never in doubt. Be positive and hopeful.

Twenty would have been a useful age to figure all of this out.

The Fourth Thing I Wish I Knew

Half the World is Starving to Death while the Other Half Seems to be on a Diet

At 20, it never occurred to me that we live in a give/get universe, and the more we give, the more we seem to get. It also did not cross my mind that half of the world has nothing while the other half has it all.

Sometimes, it seems to me that we are merely chimpanzees who have learned to use keyboards.

Yes, we have acquired skills to do amazing things, but we have cheated the evolutionary process, which generally slows things down, so our skills are in sync with our wisdom.

We seem to have landed ourselves in the middle of the technological age without the insight as to how to use it to the benefit of all of Gaia's inhabitants.

With the power of technology, we have the capacity to destroy planets and star systems but not the wisdom to realise that we operate better as a collective. It all works better when we share, care for each other on a macro scale, and utilise the opportunities offered by a diverse gene pool as we trundle blindly off into an unknown future.

Our individual instinct for survival is so strong that we cannot see the big picture. The planet has limited resources, and our ingenuity creates opportunities for using those resources more effectively, but I sometimes wonder if we are not ensuring the death of the very thing that might save us in 25,000 years' time.

Others argue that we should not plan. Rather, we should improvise when we get there. I feel like we should do both: plan all you can but have an open mind and strategies to deal with the unforeseen.

Sometimes, the way we waste the developed world's resources feels immoral in that we do not think of the other half of the planet.

We can leave it up to Gaia to sort things out, but we may not like how she does it.

At 20, none of these ideas occurred to me.

The Fifth Thing I Wish I Knew

There is a Very Large Elephant in my Room

(Let's talk a bit more about slavery and the post-slavery African diaspora.)

irst of all, let me give thanks and praise to our ancestors who survived slavery long enough to create the next generation so that we might exist. They would have come and gone unheralded like most ancestors, mythical beings, handed down through the generations until they became grainy pictures in the minds of their descendants, akin to footprints in a sandstorm. Our ancestors who lived through the slavery years fill me with great sadness that comes from knowing that any potential they might have had as they travelled the nine months from conception to birth canal was not realised.

The idea that a human being is a slave even while still attached to its mother's umbilical cord is one of the most unbearable things I have ever come across. Before that child is born, before it takes the first suck on its mother's teat, even before its conception, the potential of that child is enslaved. I shudder when I think about it, imagining that child as if it were my own.

When we talk about slavery, I sometimes feel like there is a misunderstanding about what that actually means. Here is one definition:

Slavery is a legal or economic system that uses principles of property law to classify humans as property to be owned, bought, or sold accordingly. The slaves cannot unilaterally withdraw from the arrangement. While a person is enslaved, the owner is entitled to the productivity of their labour for free. The person may become a slave from the time of his capture, purchase, or birth, until his death. In the version of slavery adopted by the Europeans, unlike some of the previous versions, an unborn child was also the property of the owner, which could have kept slavery going forever.

I am a descendant of slaves. I am the result of slavery. I am neither ashamed of it, nor am I proud of it; it just is. Slavery across the Atlantic was the starting point of a new and perilous journey that nature initiated a few hundred years ago. I am in the middle of that journey, and the final destination is unknown.

Whether you believe in Nature, Yahweh, the Universe, or whatever you think is worth worshipping or giving praise, you must recognise that something fundamental started in 1441 when the European slave trade in Africa began. Portuguese captains Antão Gonçalves and Nuno Tristão captured 12 Africans in Cabo Branco (modern Mauritania) and took them to Portugal as slaves.

Below is a timeline marking the beginning and end to the Transatlantic Slave Trade. I have done my best to incoproate all key figures and main events to the best of my knowledge. If I have left any significant contibutors out in error, my apologies.

Full acknowledgement is given to the sources for these timelines. The main acknowledgements are given to Brycchan Carey's website, The George Beattie Project's website, and jicolerenaissance.wordpress.com/portugal-the-african-slave-trade

Transatlantic Slave Trade Timeline

- In 1441, European slave trading in Africa began when two Portuguese captains, Antão Gonçalves and Nuno Tristão, kidnapped 12 Africans in Cabo Branco (modern-day Mauritania) and took them to Portugal as slaves.

- In 1444, Lançarote de Freitas, a collector of taxes from the seaside town of Lagos, Portugal, creates a company specifically to trade in Africa, and on the 8th August 1444, brings 235 kidnapped and enslaved Africans to Lagos. It is the first large group of African slaves brought to Europe.

- The year 1452 sees the start of the "sugar-slave" connection. Sugar is planted on the Portuguese island of Madeira, and for the first time, African slaves are forced to work on the sugar plantations.

- On the 18th June 1452, Pope Nicholas V – the pope of the Catholic Church – gets in on the act when he issues "Dum Diversas", a bill allowing the Portuguese to downgrade any non-Christians to the status of slaves.

- Not satisfied with the "Dum Diversas", Pope Nicholas V issues the "Romanus Pontifex" in January of 1454. This bill grants the Portuguese unending domination of trade with Africa. Nevertheless, Spanish traders begin bringing slaves from Africa to Spain.

- From 1481-86, Diogo da Azambuja erects a fortress at Elmina in what is now Ghana, which ultimately becomes the biggest and most notorious of slave-trading forts in West Africa. It is interesting to note that the first European building erected in Sub-Saharan Africa is a slave fort.

- On the 12th October 1492, Christopher Columbus, thinking he was near India, "discovers" the "Americas". If the Indigenous Americans could have peered into the future, they may have prayed harder to their gods.

- In 1509, Columbus's son, Diego Cólon, is appointed governor of the developing Spanish empire in the West Indies. He grumbles that Indigenous people are lazy and good for nothing.

- The 22nd January 1510 is the start of the organised transport of African slaves to the Americas.

- In 1527, sugar production starts in Jamaica under the Spanish and rapidly spreads across the Caribbean region. The mills are almost entirely worked by African slaves.

- In October of 1562, John Hawkins has the honour of being the first known English sailor to go about acquiring African slaves, taking some 300 from Sierra Leone and selling them in the West Indies.

- As well as starting the English slave trade, Hawkins also introduced both the potato and tobacco to England.

- In 1618, King James I of Bible fame sets up The Company of Adventurers of London Trading to the Ports of Africa. This organisation is more commonly known as The Guinea Company, the first private company to colonise Africa for profit.

- In 1655, England takes control of Jamaica from Spain.

- Also in 1655, escaped Jamaican slaves develop Maroon settlements in the Blue Mountains.

- In 1657, Juan de Bolas, a Jamaican leader of escaped slaves (Maroons) surrenders to the British but on terms of pardon and freedom. Other Maroons continue to fight British rule.

- In 1690, there is a major slave revolt in Jamaica.
- In 1699, some 75% to 85% of the Caribbean population is of enslaved Africans.
- In 1730, Britain becomes the largest slave-trading nation.
- From 1730-39, the First Maroon War in Jamaica takes place. The British agree on a treaty with Maroon leader Cudjoe in 1739, giving the Maroons 1,500 acres of land in return for helping capture other escaped slaves.
- In the 1770s, abolitionist campaigner Granville Sharpe collects evidence showing that slavery is incompatible with English law.
- In 1775, a royal commission is set up to gather evidence on the slave trade.
- In 1781, the Zong case – in which some 470 African people are forced onto the slave ship Zong – causes outrage and reinforces the abolition campaign. The conditions are so appalling that seven crew members and 60 Africans die from sickness, and some 133 sick Africans are thrown overboard and left to drown. The case is heard as an insurance dispute, not a murder trial.
- 1789 marks the publication of Olaudah Equiano's *The Interesting Narrative of the Life of Olaudah Equiano, or Gustavus Vassa, the African.*

- Also in 1789, William Wilberforce presents the first abolition bill to the House of Commons, although it does not pass.

- A slave revolt in St. Domingue in 1791 begins the Haitian Revolution in which Toussaint L'Ouverture leads a multitude of ex-slaves. The revolution eventually leads to the island becoming an independent Haiti in 1804.

- In 1831, a major slave rebellion, called The Baptists' War, breaks out in Jamaica, led by Baptist preacher Sam Sharpe, which is brutally suppressed.

- 1833 marks the establishment of the Abolition of Slavery Act, after which Britain stops slavery and prepares for the release of enslaved people in the British West Indies. Set to take effect in August 1834, the Act announces that the formerly incarcerated people must serve six years of apprenticeship before receiving full emancipation. Though this period is initially set to six years, it is later reduced to four.

- In 1838, the apprentice system is abolished following peaceful protests in Trinidad, guaranteeing the complete emancipation of all former slaves in the colonies.

- 1865 marks the biggest and most famous revolt by black Jamaicans in which 17 Europeans are killed, and 32 are injured after a riot in Morant Bay, in which the crowd attacks the police station and local militia. Many plantations are also attacked over the course of a few days.

The authorities, as usual, overreact and declare martial law. The ringleaders are executed, and around 400 black people are murdered.

- In 1888, slavery is finally abolished in Brazil, the largest Portuguese-speaking country in the world and the last state in the Western world to eliminate it.

These realities that have made me have also denied me and what I ought to have been from ever becoming real.

That me drifted off into a parallel universe where, hopefully, I grew up in the love, security, and traditions of the past thousand years in the river beds, plains, and valleys of West Africa.

The new me, after all this time, will look you in the eye and proudly say: I was, I am, and I will become again what I was always intended to be.

We people from the Caribbean came to England on the *Windrush* to help the "mother" country get back on her feet after the war with Germany, and our "mother" waited for us with open arms, or, at least, that's what we were told. The reality, however, was a little different.

At 20, I was still naive as to how deep the post-slavery mentality ran. I had not realised that if I were a victim, then so were the white people being stifled and ultimately spoiled by the privilege of privilege.

Privilege stops you from wanting to keep going. You convince yourself there is someone worse off than you, someone who you can look down, someone who will be blamed for most things in your society so you can keep your head down and all will be okay. That is the penalty of privilege – it stops you from using pressure as a tool for improvement.

In 1965, we were not aware of the effect of enslavement on the UK's post-slavery citizens. Small things went on, such as the middle- and upper-class men and women of the UK, categorising black people below the working class regardless of their status in their home country. This racism had a profound effect on some of the young men who came over from the Caribbean in the early sixties. One particular victim still haunts me.

I first met him in 1965, at the Labour Exchange in Spurstow Terrace in Hackney. He was playing the fool, making a lot of noise as he waited to collect his unemployment benefits. He was young, there was life in his future, and he was just fooling around and doing nothing until he got the job of his dreams. He would not work for no Backra (Boss Man) – his ideas would take him places. He obviously could not live on the pittance he was being given – he could only afford chicken back – but he was okay, living at his parents' home with no bills to pay.

I was lucky. The Royal Navy came to my rescue, and I did not see him again until 1971 when I left the navy and went to the unemployment office to sign on again. He was still there, making the same noises to assure himself he was still alive, and I realised the place was contaminated, and if I stayed,

I, too, would be stained with the lethargy and hopelessness I witnessed, and I never went back.

In that moment, I realised that Britain gives you the pittance to stop you from being a nuisance. If you could reduce your spending to the point where you could live on the benefits, then the children of the wealthy could carry on eating steaks and drinking Champagne, and you would carry on blaming yourself for your continued failure.

I did not know any of this at 20.

The Sixth Thing I Wish I Knew

Racism will still be Around in the 21st Century

At Christmas of 2012, I was home. It was a quiet afternoon, one when the wife and kids had escaped the house with the sole mission of hunting down bargains in London. In my hunger for solitude, I had found some reason for staying home with the phone off the hook and a small sherry as my only companion, and I started to reflect.

By then, I was quite ill with chronic heart disease caused by ventricular tachycardia and a host of other issues, including chronic lung disease caused by Amiodarone, the drug that was used to keep me alive while the doctors desperately searched for a long-term solution to the tachycardia. Funny thing, life – sometimes, the very thing keeping you alive is also killing you. I was not supposed to drink the sherry, but I did so anyway. I mean, what could it do – slay me again? I had already died two or three times over the past ten years.

It was in one of those moments when I was reflecting on my life, the journey, and significant influences (you know, the people who made me get up to say something about my people's position, what I was going to do about it, and how I was going to help) that I remembered the work of Bob Marley and Curtis Mayfield, especially *Redemption Song* and *We People Who Are Darker Than Blue*.

The following is the culmination of those thoughts:

I know that in these precarious times, silence is the best guarantee of a safe, quiet, and peaceful tomorrow. I wonder, though, if we haven't been silent for too long. I also wonder how long we should just keep accepting our tomorrows, whether they suit us or not. When do we start positively shaping the tomorrows our children will inherit? When do we stop hiding ourselves away so that no one knows who we really are, thereby denying our children the positive role models for which they cry out?

Stephen Lawrence's justice came, begrudgingly and almost with a great deal of reluctance, and the press immediately found something to divert the nation's thoughts away from the real issues.

"Ah, well, racism is very complex – some of our black MPs are racists as well," says the cynical racism denier. This was entirely predictable – but I digress.

I have read the strategies developed to keep the slaves under control. I mean, they had to have a plan because, on some of the plantations, there were under ten white men controlling 200 to 300 slaves.

The strategies used by the owners under the approval of their home countries were to:

- Keep the black men physically strong and mentally weak.

- Give the slaves no rights under the law and have a strong and brutal militia close by.

- Heap a level of unprecedented terrorism on the slaves, including violence, rape and humiliation, and ensure that other slaves witnessed it as a reminder of what could happen to them if they misbehaved.

- Tell them that they were all right, but the other slave was from another tribe, island, village, faith, etc., and could not be trusted.

- Kill any slave found trying to learn to read and/or write; education of the slaves was what frightened the slavers the most.

- See all slaves as subhuman, allowing them to beat, maim, and/or kill the slaves with impunity.

- Sell children, wives, and mothers to let the men know they had no power whatsoever, and if they did not toe the line, worst things could happen to them.
- Treat black human beings as chattel to be bought and sold or given away as gifts.

People who say they cannot understand how ten white men could keep so many black men under their control have naively suggested that the slaves were cowards. What is not visible 200-300 years later is the level of brutality used to subjugate them. The level of violence was unprecedented in modern times. Children were taught fear from a very early age. They would see their relatives hanged, drawn and quartered, and whipped until the flesh fell from their backs, and their mothers raped, cut up, and fed to the dogs, and they would be cowed for a lifetime.

Mothers watched their children sold to other plantations, raped at five or six, and if the child died, the mother was told to get pregnant again. Their hearts would turn to stone, and they, too, would be cowed for a lifetime.

The men hid their hearts and minds and became physically strong and mentally weak. The brutality of their existence and their natural survival instincts almost destroyed their humanity and their ability to care for their loved ones, and they, too, would be cowed for generations.

What it did to the people who perpetrated these crimes and their descendants, we will never know.

The legacy of this strategy is that for nearly 160 years, we have been handed down these fears by our post-slavery forefathers through AUTOPOIESIS (See the Lamarckian inheritance[1]: direct transfer of lifetime learning results to offspring).

So, now, we trust any other race to build our houses, fix our cars, look after our money in the bank, but we do not trust our own. Why?

It is because we have been told that we are useless and cannot do anything well, so how can anyone who looks like us be any good at anything? Like crabs in a barrel, we fight to ensure that all our crabs stay powerless.

Some laugh at us and sell us anything they want because we still believe that it must be good if it comes from them. Others sell us things and follow us about the shop, making sure we do not steal anything.

Divide and conquer strategies keep us fighting each other. Some of our lighter-skinned brothers and sisters still think they are superior to our darker-skinned brothers and sisters. Still. In 2020.

Different islanders from the Caribbean call each other derogatory names even though 300 years ago, they may have come from the same West African village. We have to stop this now. The time for change is now.

---

1 Lamarckian inheritance, also known as "Neo-Lamarckism", is the notion that an organism can pass on to its offspring physical characteristics that the parent organism acquired through use or disuse during its lifetime.

What are we going to do about it?

- Honour our past. Recognise it for what it was: the creation of us and the beginning of the third wave of men coming out of Africa to make the world a different place.

- Further educate ourselves so that we find better solutions to our problems.

- Trade with each other until we can no longer provide the services required.

- See our journeys as a part of fulfilling the Book.

- Recognise that it is always darkest before the dawn.

- Stay strong, mentally and physically.

- Stay in harmony with nature and your God.

- Remember that the more pressure you put on a piece of coal, the better the diamond it becomes.

- In the grand scheme of things, this is merely HUMANITY evolving.

- Finally, and probably most critically: we need to REDEFINE what success means to the African diaspora in the 21st century. We have spent the last 400 years trying to become a black copy of the Caucasian, almost as if we want to be the best Caucasians we can be. Is this what we really want? To replace our previous masters? Do we want to become their slave masters? Isn't there more for us to achieve? Are we not better than that? I believe that we are spiritual beings, and Gaia is applying pressure to us to make us evolve beyond the limits of a Neo-Roman Capitalist led civilisation.

How do we go about changing things?

- Talk to each other. Let each other know the skills, talents, and opportunities we bring to the table.

- Put together a leaflet, database, or circular to let each other know about the talents we have discovered.

- Begin to love ourselves so that we can respect, love, and have faith in others who look like us.

- There are no such things as Smallies, Biggies, bad Jamaicans, or sneaky Puerto Ricans; there are only people trying to get through the day. These lies designed to divide and conquer were created by people trying to corrupt our psyche. Stop believing them.

- Remember Juan de Bolas, Mada Nanny, and Toussaint L'Ouverture, who forged a united team of slaves who took on the might of the Spanish, French, and British and defeated them. United, we are strong.

- Create a strong economic force by making sure we trade with each other first, second, third, fourth, and fifth. Support anyone who tries to develop our economy. The most successful ethnic groups trade amongst themselves seven times before letting others see their money. The second most successful groups do it five times. Afro-Caribbeans and Afro-Americans do it less than 0.5 times at the moment. This is the major problem we face right now. It is why we are laughed at and not taken seriously by some. We have to create a business and economic infrastructure to change this.

- Teach the children so they can pass on the positive lessons of the past and present to the next generation.

- Get your children educated. Help them choose professions that will enhance themselves and us at the same time. Fifteen percent of our Asian brothers and sisters have a degree. A significant number of them go into professions where their numbers make them strong. We must emulate them.

- This journey is at least four generations long. There is no superhero to change things at the speed of light. There is only us, doing it daily, remorselessly.

- We must learn what we don't know and what we need to know.

- Marcus Garvey's Black Star Line was systematically destroyed by people who wanted to maintain control over how we spend our money.

What things do we need to hold on to?

- Remember that we are good people who have had bad things done to us.

- These bad things are still being done today.

- We must remember who we were and hold onto who we will become.

- That the journey will make us diamonds, and we are about to shine.
- Why our parents and grandparents came to England, Canada, or the USA.

What things do we need to leave behind?
- The pain of humiliation.
- The fear and lack of confidence our ancestors passed on to us, and we pass on to our children.
- The idea that we are not intelligent enough to think deep and complex thoughts.
- The fear of being educated – we won't be murdered for it in 2020.
- The fear of failure and getting it wrong.
- The lack of love, empathy, and trust we display for ourselves and people who look like us.

Who do we need to emulate?
- People who strive to have 15% of their community with a university degree.
- People who have a strong sense of their history, the good bits and the bad.
- People who spend their money within their community six or seven times before anyone else sees it.
- People who believe in themselves and their God.
- That tomorrow is going to be a good day.

What new things do we need to learn and make happen?

- You cannot trust anyone else with your children's future.
- You have to take personal responsibilities for their education, well-being, and development.
- The most important thing a mother can give her child is an excellent father and vice versa – be choosy; be selective.
- We are evolving beings, so evolve.

How do we get rid of our fears?

- By staring them in the face and doing what you know to be right.
- If you are not afraid of the consequence, the fear melts away.
- When it becomes unbearable, say to yourself, "This, too, shall pass," and carry on.

The Seventh Thing I Wish I Knew

The Past is a Temporary but Relevant Place

What has the last 570 years of evolution done to make us different? At no other time in human history has there been such a concentrated coming together of all strands in the human gene pool as there has been in the Caribbean over the last 500-600 years. What changes are being made to the human-animal as a result of these transmutations?

The people of the Caribbean Sea may just represent the next phase of evolution in the human experiment.

At no time in the history of humans since we began our first migratory journey out of Africa 1,000,000 years ago has there been such a resilient, cohesive reconnection of the building blocks of humanity as we see in this area at this specific moment in time.

Chinese, Indian, Japanese, Caucasian, Jewish, African, Olmec, Taino, Arawak, and other original Indigenous people from the American continent are all together in this tiny part of the world in the Caribbean Sea. Add to this the survival of the fittest strategy which must have been used by nature to ensure that at least some of us survived the great number of deaths on the journey. If we add 400 years of enforced slavery into the mix, we may just be witnessing the start of humanity's new journey. Nature usually has a plan. This was the case way before humans had awoken.

If there is a new journey to be made, we still want to bring our kids up to be bright, super-fit, super-intelligent inheritors of our past, but does this past have to be the old Greco-Roman, capitalist way of seeing the world and doing things? Is this what we want?

Do we really want to go through the journey, only to have our children look down on others and see themselves as somehow superior to other humans? Do we want them to believe they are entitled to all the benefits of the planet merely because they were born to a particular family, person, genetic disposition, or moment in our brief history? Or do we want their characters and abilities to define their successes?

Do we want them to help Gaia create a better, more peaceful, life-affirming, humane, unselfish way of managing the planet for all its inhabitants? This, it seems to me, is our next great philosophical debate as we continue to evolve.

I wish I understood and had all of this assimilated at 20!

The Eighth Thing I Wish I Knew

Sometimes, You Really have to Pray Because there is Nothing Left to do

I am not a profoundly religious man. I think that God has a lot to answer for, and if He were to suddenly turn up in the skies, I would be surprised that multitudinous thought control can make things happen before your very eyes. But I have faith in the goodness and hopefulness of life.

I usually keep my thoughts on spirituality, religion, mindfulness, and philosophy very much to myself. However, in the past decade or so, I, like many others to whom I have spoken, have felt a hardening in the intolerance of some humans to others on an emotional and maybe even a spiritual level. It is almost as if everyone is only out for themselves and all the collective accepted wisdom that has defined the goodness in us suddenly means nothing:

- Millions of people are killed in wars that rage in the Middle East and no one cares.

- People fleeing from those wars who try to get safely to Europe are referred to as cockroaches (less than human) and are abandoned. Thousands die because no one cares.

- The American Red Cross, allegedly collected $500,000,000 (yes, five hundred million dollars) from the public to help Haiti after the earthquake and apparently only managed to build six (yes, six) homes with it, and no one cares.

- Charities are now multi-national corporations with CEOs earning million-dollar salaries, without much money going towards its original intent. Does anyone care?

- United Kingdom decides to leave the European Union because most of its inhabitants think this will stop European migrants from coming to the UK. Migrants are beaten and killed on the streets of the UK, and no one cares.

- The American people have selected a man full of hate to be the president of the most dominant nation on Earth. Now, we see what hatred can do when it has power. And no one cares.

- The rich take more, the poor get left less, and the media now only defends the super-rich that pays its wages.

- The poor think they are only temporarily poor, so laws brought in to protect the needy no longer applies to them. And still, no one cares.

- The planet seems to be dying from the inside out as its heart beats slower and slower.

This prayer or reflection is sent to whatever force or energy we believe guides us on Gaia. We may need your help and guidance as hopelessness seems to be in control.

Oh, Universal Force, Yahweh, Allah, Jah, Controller of the Void (whatever designed this existence),

We come to you at this time of great need to seek your wisdom and guidance. You know what is, what was, and what will be. Your insight and advice are, therefore, supreme.

Give our minds and our words clarity so that very complex philosophical issues can be visualised, enabling us to understand what is being said and how best to implement it. Give our minds the peace required to hear the message.

Let this planet be at peace with itself. Let it be a refuge for those who need it to be, and You know who they are. Keep all our brothers and sisters (all life) safe, especially those in imminent danger.

We come to you this day with great humility, hoping that your grace and mercy will guide us as we take yet another step closer to You. In the Great War that rages between hope and hopelessness, let hope reign supreme. You know what is in our hearts, so please soothe any pain, uncertainty, anxiety, and desolation as You have always done.

As we look across the world, the chaos feels like the start of the biblical battle of Armageddon as predicted in the final book of the Christian Bible, Revelations. Nations are killing each other, tribes are killing each other, the world is hypnotised by hate, and a lot of the haters say that it is all in Your name.

Please, tell us until we understand what is going on. We know that suffering is driven by fear, and the law of "Thou Shalt Not Kill" cannot be upheld while fear casts its shadow across the world. It is time to let love fill the hearts of everything on this planet, enabling peace to reign. Let Your mighty power of love reign over us today, and give us the insight to witness You at work.

In the great turmoil that sometimes overwhelms us, let our minds be as fresh and alert as they can be. Give us all the strength to carry on, the will to do what is necessary, the courage to get through the day, and the heart to keep loving when there is no reason to.

Please, carry us and breathe for us when we do not have the strength to take the next step or to blow the next breath. Let us all have the courage to do what we know to be true. Keep us safe and at peace with ourselves, our friends, and our neighbours.

Let those who are imminently on their way to You have a safe journey and wipe away all fear as they journey through the valley of shadows. Let them have the courage to do what they know to be true.

Keep guiding us as we take one more uncertain step away from war and towards Your way of peace, love, hope, and wisdom.

Make each step more confident than the one before it, and make the final steps a mighty gallop.

Let hope be audacious and victorious. We ask all this in Your everlasting name.

The Ninth Thing I Wish I Knew

Equality and Capitalism are Fighting Each Other

At 20, I wish I knew how difficult the battle for human equality on this planet would be. It was obvious to see that it would take some time for everyone living on planet Earth to get a fair share of the spoils, but at 20, I thought that it would all be sorted out after a few years. Humans are reasonable people, and they would see the right way and do the right thing in the end.

The end is still nowhere in sight, and equality is a distant dream. What I failed to comprehend is the fear driving some of our actions. For all of us to be equal, some people have to give something up, either some of the wealth accumulated – or in some cases, stolen – over the past 1,000 years, or the knowledge we have been keeping to ourselves about how to do things. If not, then we must suspend the belief that we have as many resources as we do because we are somehow better than everyone else.

Once we stop thinking that nature has given us entitlement to the wealth, education, knowledge, etc., and that we actually might have just been lucky, we can correct the way we think the world works. The trouble is that we are selfish beings, and we confuse the strategies needed as individuals to live out the next few years and as the human race to outlive time. I think (in the end) we will find the solutions to these struggles and forget they ever existed. The trouble is that it takes millennia for this to happen, and individually, we are only allotted 70 or so years to live, so we will never be able to see the outcome.

At 20, I wish I knew that Capitalism was not the solution to humanity's woes, that in the end, it would create more problems than it could ever solve, and the only beneficiaries would be the super-rich.

Do not get me wrong: I am not poor, whatever that means. I have enough food to eat, clothes to wear, and a roof over my head. I live on a pension which I spent a lot of time and money accruing during my working years. I retired some years ago due to ill health and having reached the ripe old age of 65.

I am a baby boomer, that lucky generation of people living in the Western capitalist system born between 1945 and

1965, the golden years after the Second World War when there were a massive rebuilding and research programme based on science, technology, and capital investment.

Whatever we did turned to gold. All of our investments paid off. It did not take a great deal of skill to keep or maintain our wealth; it simply grew. We bought a house whose value increased while we slept. The price of everything came down year after year, disposable income went up, and most people could afford a house if they wanted.

Poverty in the UK during the '60s and '70s was not real poverty compared to the deprivation I witnessed in Bombay, Subic Bay, and Hong Kong, or the abject emptiness I had heard of in parts of Africa. In England, people complained about indigence without ever really knowing what it was. I ignored the empty noise as I genuinely felt that ignorance of what it was to go without food or water for days made people imagine they were worse off than they actually were. The soft belly of the welfare state had the effect of keeping the poor and unearning anaesthetised against the reality of poverty.

In the great competition between the richer and the poorer of the post-war era, the richer found ways to ensure that the poorer remained uneducated and ill-equipped to challenge their children for the spoils of the land. The poorer became reconciled, sedated, and almost asleep when it came to the aspirational possibilities presented by post-war opportunities to the Western winners of the war.

The super-rich took the acquisition of resources to another level, and between 1960 and 2016, the super-rich's grabbing of global resources became obscene. Over twenty trillion pounds of the world's resources – stolen in some cases – had been trapped and stored away in offshore funds, gold, and private banks by the super-rich, far from the prying eyes of governments and their tax officials.

This money will never again see the light of day because it will never be needed for day to day survival or expenses. This money is to ensure – or should that be insure – that these families are moneyed for the next 5,000 years. If that means that 10,000,000 people die of hunger in Africa or Asia, what concern is it of theirs?

"These poor people do not know what it is like to work hard, anyway. They sit all day, waiting for someone to hand them something to eat. These poorer people are like cockroaches who are not fit to be in the same species as the winners," say the super-rich and their sycophants.

People escaping from war created by the super-rich to make more money were decried as immigrants by the West, terrorists, and other negative stereotypes to set the poor to fighting amongst themselves.

Slowly, the middle-classes were destroyed by the power of the super-rich, so in the end, only the super-rich and the serfs will remain.

No one wanted to be seen as hard up, so everyone thought of themselves as "temporarily poor". This absence of ownership made sure that all the systems in place to help people with low income were ridiculed or killed off by the very people for which they were originally intended. The middle-classes were so busy making sure the poorer ones did not bridge the gap between them that they failed to see how far the super-rich were leaving them behind.

The poorer – who were kept uninformed as a part of the "killing off of the competition" programme – did what they always do: they had long ago given up on blaming the rich for anything, as it had always given them more problems than it was worth. They still, however, needed someone to blame for their ills, and the easy target was someone who was even worse off than them.

Imagine blaming someone with even less power than you for your problems. If they were that powerful, surely, they would not be worse off than you. When you are kept uninformed and uneducated, logic escapes and flees in exasperation.

I could have done with that insight at 20

The Tenth Thing I Wish I Knew

Some Needs can Never be Satiated

It would have been beneficial if I had known that I should not allow other people's moods and behaviours to affect my values and the way I view and do things. I wasted a lot of my life trying to please others, trying to make sure everyone else was okay, and I would only make do with the leftovers of my time, energy, and other resources, once I had satisfied their needs. My needs never seemed to be satiated, but that was okay because I felt that I was doing great good. The friends, acquaintances, and relatives I was out there helping never seemed satiated either, and their needs were a constant drain on my energy.

Never once did I get the impression that they had all the help they needed and were now gracefully grateful for my support. Instead, I was left thinking that they had said, "What have you done for me lately?" too many times for me ever to be satisfied with what I had done for them. I was also very distracted by the moods and reactions some people had to ensure their plans were prioritised.

In my generous mood, I thought I had all the time in the world to do whatever anyone wanted from me and what I wanted for myself. As it turned out, I did not have the time, and illness has made sure that some of these grand ideas will never come to fruition. And yet, when I look at some of the dreams I have helped others fulfil, I cannot help but be proud. If I remember all of this in the next life, I will follow the universal values inside my heart.

But I do wonder why I needed to be so obsessive about helping others, even when I was 20.

The Eleventh Thing I Wish I Knew

Blind Faith Can Give You Incongruous Belief Systems

At 20, I truly believed that science had all the answers the universe would ultimately establish as the ultimate truth about everything. I reasoned that, in science, man had found a way of conceiving, testing, and proving all things, ideas, and notions that we, as a species, could ever come up with. I imagined that one plus one would always make two, whether you were on Earth, Alpha Centauri, or in the furthermost universe in the multitude of universes that may exist.

At 70, I am not as sure, and I think that the study of philosophy may find more absolute truths than science ever could.

Do not get me wrong – I still think of science as a rough and ready guide of how things are and how they should be, which is a great tool to open the doors to ideas and concepts. But some things are unprovable now and will remain so forever, so you ultimately have to go back to the maxim that if you can conceive it in your imagination, then it can be achieved.

It seems to me that there is a deep connection between thought and how and why things are created, that the imagination is a far greater universal force than that for which we give credit. I feel that this energy source is directly connected to the centre of all energy sources in all the universes, and the subject that understands it most is philosophy, the study of THINKING.

Our belief systems are some of the most sophisticated thought processes ever created, far more complex than Boolean algebra, more demanding than superstring theory, and with no basis in scientific theory. They have failed nearly every test ever asked of them, and still, we believe.

We believe in a GOD. We believe in the goodness of humanity, the same humanity that has murdered millions of other humans, and we still have faith in the overwhelming goodness of our species.

There is no tangible proof and no evidence that a god or God exists or has ever existed, no definable, physical verification that goodness and evil, souls, devils, and angels or archangels are out there in the vastness of our universes, yet our minds have conceived them and created them for a purpose only it knows.

When studying thinking, we can say that thought was created to implant and/or overcome fears that come from our inability to control our enemies, ourselves, and our environments.

We could, in fact, argue that everything we touch, feel, see, hear, and taste is a figment of our imagination, put there by the conceptualising chemicals of our mind's eye, and nothing is real.

Alternatively, if our imagination can conceive anything and everything and then achieve it, then everything is real, and the study of thinking holds the key to unlocking how and what everything is. Maybe, just maybe, God or gods, devils, good, bad, angels, spirits, souls, white magic, black magic, travelling faster than the speed of light, and overcoming time are all real and possible. We just have to tap into the right part of the imagination to make them real. The brain is an evolving, intellectual storehouse – it may be a universe in its own right. The most advanced humans use only about ten per cent of their brains' intellectual and intelligence capacity – what might the other 90% do?

I wish I had these answers now I am 70, never mind when I was 20.

The Twelfth Thing I Wish I Knew

The Most Important Things in Life are the Relationships we Create

As a father, the most important thing you can give your child is a good mother, someone who will help them become the best they can be. Someone who, through your mutual love and understanding, will give your child a picture of the world that will nourish them and an environment in which they can grow. No single parent can do this on his or her own. In my view, it takes two parents to get the best in and out of their children. I am not saying that a single parent will not do well; they will just not do as well as two parents with the same aim.

The structure of a family must start with the parents. They must come first. They create the way the family works. Mothers and/or fathers who put their children first upset the natural order of things, and there will be consequences waiting for them in the future.

If a man puts the children ahead of his wife, the children will start to see their mother as less, not worthy, someone whose values, ideas, and contributions to their development and welfare as being not as significant as the father's. In my view, this action is the same as when the mother treats the father as less significant than the children – it carries on into future generations as an anomaly that never gets resolved.

It is essential that parents bring emotional maturity to the table when they have children – this is the cornerstone upon which relationships are built. The environment the family creates as they nurture the young ones from cradle to maturity will be the most significant input into the way the children's lives turn out.

Their love and respect for each other must be unconditional; however, adults and children alike have to understand that every action has a consequence, and you must be prepared to live with the after-effects when you act.

The balancing act between your role as a parent and that as your spouse's lover can be so complicated that it sometimes leads to resentment. These changes in our needs, values and views can threaten the love we thought was sacrosanct, the love that may just be declining. Love comes in many ways and guises and differing times. If it ends, do not give up, keep your hopes high.

Try not to chase love; it will come to you when it is good and ready. You will not find love; it will track you, down. Sometimes it will find you at a nightclub with an energy that touches you. A spirit instinctively connects with you, you scan the room, and your eyes meet. Another time, you might e halfway down an escalator, look across at the travellers 'ng up, and catch the glare of someone looking at you with rmidable intent so overwhelming that it feels as if the 'y has emanated from that person to touch your soul. be the right person at the wrong time, the start of an i ion period, or even life giving you an insight into the te e of that for which you are looking.

times, in our loneliness and fear, we convince ours s that this is the right person when we know, deep down here it matters, that it is not. We run out of patience and downgrade the importance of getting it right. We say yes when we should be saying no, and five years later, we are alone again with a broken heart and a mind full of grief.

When the love is right, there are seldom any problems – the flow is positive, the conversations anxiety-free, and the laughter pours like water from an endless stream.

Do not fight it when love dies. Love is not yours. It is not something you can keep under lock and key with 24-hour security protecting it. The great thing about love is that it is like the wind: it is free, it is unconditional, and when it is with you, it is because it wants to be. Be honoured that you were worthy of it. It comes, it goes, it comes again. Hate is the result when you try to make a prisoner of love.

Love requires energy to sustain itself. It is not necessarily a frenetic energy. Sometimes it is quiet and peaceful, depending on who is involved.

I am probably an introvert. Sometimes, I use a persona that has people believing that I am an intelligent, enigmatic character, full of wisdom and deep understanding. In truth, I am undoubtedly a shy guy who creates a façade able to do the dirty work called communication, especially when I am on stage and speaking to a crowd. In small groups of ten or so people who I do not know very well, I tend to find reasons to escape the awkward gaps and pregnant pauses plaguing so many conversations.

I do not do quiet tête-à-têtes. They seem to run out of energy halfway through, and the pauses just hang there until you find an excuse to scuttle off to safety or find another victim with whom to share one more charged hiatus. Me, I just move along to my next assignment and leave the pregnant pauses to others.

My son, a sagacious young man, told me that an introvert uses energy to communicate, and an extrovert gets energy from communicating. I immediately understood what he meant by that.

We cannot create or sustain positive relationships without secure and loving communication. It is an essential part, whether you are an extrovert or an introvert. The approach, however, might be different.

I think I was brought up to be suspicious of over-emotional people and what they bring to a relationship. I am a bit restrained, a bit tight – the way my father and his father and his father before him were. This is what it is like to be a man. It stifles me, but it also relieves me from taking part in deeply emotional chit chat. In the end, my restraint confines me to peer at relationships through the envelopes, unable to read the letters. They leave me wounded but uninformed as to why. I wish I could get my hands and feet dirty in the nitty-gritty of feelings evoked by emotions, but my father never taught me how, and I am afraid to start learning now.

By the time we get to 60, we have created survival zones in which we are comfortable and which we seldom leave. They protect us; they only reinforce what we already know and like. Any new ideas and/or thoughts are like barbarians knocking at the fortress gate, trying to get in. We resist them with an ardour not seen since our youth when we thought all things were possible and transformative. We do this, I think, because we are afraid of old age, a reduced quality of life, and finally, death, and we build a fortification to keep out uncertainty. The only problem with this is that the universe exists to change and everything solidifies and become unwieldy without these adjustments.

This information would have been extremely handy at 20.

The Thirteenth Thing I Wish I Knew

The Story about the Caterpillar and the Butterfly

At 20, I wish I knew there would come a time when humans naturally evolve into personas that the previous inhabitants of their body will not recognise. It is a bit like a caterpillar growing into a butterfly.

A caterpillar does not know it is destined to be a butterfly or a moth. It thinks that all it has to do is eat, so it eats and eats. It gets big; it sleeps. It does not plan for a life as a butterfly. It thinks that all it will be called upon to do for all of its existence is crawl on its legs and hunt food.

It loves its round, cylindrical body and the way it moves around the fields, eating anything it can get into its mouth.

It plans to live its entire life as a crawler on the ground. Sometimes, it sees a butterfly drinking nectar from the top of a tree, and it laughs at the energy it must waste, merely to get food. It is not impressed by the butterfly's ability to see more in a day than it will see in a lifetime. The caterpillar sees its world and all that is in it, and it is filled with contentment.

Sometimes, it may see a large bird fly off to distant lands and get slightly annoyed that it has to remain within 100 yards of its place of birth, but the feeling soon goes away when the next meal presents itself.

It has not given it much thought, but it knows, deep down, that when it finds a way to produce children, they will look like it, act like it, and so it goes on, ad infinitum. They will die, looking and behaving like it. This is just the way things are. None of us can change the way we look and think! We are what we see in the mirror every day.

The caterpillar's strategy, if a caterpillar has one, is that it "knows" how its body operates. After a couple of months, it knows all there is to know about itself and any assumptions it makes about itself is based on this early knowledge and any empirical insights gained about what it is. It assumes its maturation will be simple because it has never seen a caterpillar transforming into a butterfly.

Then, one night, it goes to sleep, and after what seems like a quick nap, although it is between five and twenty one days, it wakes to find itself a butterfly with no memory of what it once was and how to live its life.

Then, it looks up at the sky and just flies away.

Some mornings, I wake up, look deeply into the mirror, and the butterfly staring back is not someone I recognise at all.

At 20-years-old, I wish I knew this would happen to me, but I wonder if it would have made a difference. I simply and honestly do not know.

an implication for me and likely someone else. Sometimes, if I were lucky, the effects were targeted, intentional, and appropriate. In most cases, the consequences were unintended, and like ripples in a rivulet – they just kept going until I knew I was no longer in control of them.

At 70, I try to figure out the obvious consequences of my significant actions. Sometimes, I am so consumed by avoiding unintended consequences that I am frozen to inaction and become so afraid of getting it wrong that I do nothing.

I have learnt to just do things as long as I can assure myself that no one will die.

The Fifteenth Thing I Wish I Knew

You Cannot do Anything to Help Someone Until They Decide They Need it

*I*n my younger days – around about the age of 20 – when I was filled with the confidence – no, the arrogance of the uninformed – I thought I could help anyone see sense, whether they wanted to or not.

I thought my persuasive skills could show my friends and family the error of their ways, and that I could teach them the skills, sayings, and ideas I had picked up along the way.

I had the confidence of youth and thought that my journeys around the world had filled my head with wisdom as opposed to little maps of obscure, small places scattered around the globe. I started to believe my verbiage, and after a while, became annoyed if someone had the temerity to question my insights. How dare they develop doubts or decline the solution I proposed? Did they not know who I was? Their need was great, and if they did not want my help, then that was on them.

It took me a long while to appreciate that people are proud, dignified, and want to sort out their problems themselves. It gives us all great encouragement to have a problem and come up with its solution. No one wants to feel obligated to someone else for bailing them out, regardless of the size of the bail.

Now, I know, and I always remember that people have to reach the bottom, that place without hope, before they recognise they need help and ask for it. You cannot help anyone until then.

The Sixteenth Thing I Wish I Knew

Patience and Understanding also has a Role in My Life

My life would be different if, at 20, I knew that the journey of life requires great patience and profound understanding.

It seems as if life is not very complicated at 20 — you get up in the morning and do what needs to be done to put food on the table. If you cannot do it, then your parent or guardian will do it for you as you still rely on them for your survival, when push comes to shove. Your body is a temple you worship, and the opposite sex is a pleasure dome.

You are told that there could be consequences if you are not careful and do not protect yourself, like having a child for which you are not ready for. Your body, however, has different ideas about that for which you are prepared. As far as it is concerned, you have been equipped since you were 14 or so, and all it wants to do is prove that you are a man. Consequently, by 20 or so, the boys who have not had "the conversation" with their trusted, wiser friends, older brothers, or as a final event, their parents, are there, waiting outside maternity wards for the arrival of their firstborn. They are too young to do the best thing they can as a father for their children, which is to make sure they find them the best mother they can. They stumble from then on, from one problem to another, and life just gets complicated.

Take your time at 20. Time is all you have. Life will still be there, along with everything else, at 30.

It is great to have a plan, but life is the thing that unfolds itself as you are planning it, so be pliable, tolerant, and flexible with changes you impose on others and those that others impose on you. Some of them will help along the way; others will not.

Trust people until they prove they cannot be trusted. Do not allow the prejudices and assumptions of your forefathers and foremothers to dominate or get in the way of the relationships or decisions you will make in your time.

These hand me down rules, hates, dislikes, and ways of behaviour were never really acceptable in some cases and were undoubtedly not conceived with you in mind. They were created out of the immediacy, hate, and fear of another time. Have a look at them and scrutinise them from top to bottom before deciding if they are of any use to you. Do not assume that someone different than you is automatically better – or worse, inferior – or should just take a back seat.

If you have to make assumptions, try to make them positive. Only assume that something is negative when it has proven itself to be negative.

Treat each life as a new day, and each decision as a unique opportunity, a new chance to review what our ancestors have told us and begin again.

At some point along your journey, you have to take responsibility for who you are to become. Your parents, guardians, and/or relatives might have done things in the past that have shaped you and made you who you are, but at some point, you have to bury those things and move on, or you will not succeed. I think that, by the time you are 25 or 30, you can carry on, wallowing in self-pity and blind fury, or even use the distress of your youth as a reason for the inertia. You could also say to yourself, "It is my time now, and I am going to be what I want to be." The choice is yours.

20 is a really good time to start figuring this out.

The Seventeenth Thing I Wish I Knew

Not all Problems will Cause You Woe

ometimes, I wonder if we are trying to prevent the world from becoming what it is destined to become. Other times, in the depths of certainty, I realise that I am powerless to create right from wrong, light from dark, or even right from left.

Why do I worry so much about what others are doing? I am not in control of anything, including myself. If the world is going left, I should only worry if I want to go right.

I really ought to try to go with the flow as not all problems will cause me woe.

I am fed up with people hiding their actions in the brightest of light, denying it in plain view, as if our eyes are blind, our ears deaf, and our nose incapable of smelling the truth.

Sometimes, my fears and uncertainty overwhelm the very things I love, but nothing can harm you if you worry less and care more. It's not always your fault when it all goes wrong, so don't worry; be happy. Go with the flow. Not all problems will cause you woe.

Things are only a problem when they become a problem. Until then, they are just possibilities that don't exist.

That not all problems would cause me woe would have been good to know at 20.

The Eighteenth Thing I Wish I Knew

Life Owes You Nothing

When I was 20, it never occurred to me that life was not in my control, that although I was living it, it was only on loan, a kind of leasehold as opposed to a freehold, and at some point in the future (sometimes distant, other times not too distant), I would have to give it all back.

I thought that life was something I could bend to my will, a tool I had to measure my time on this planet called Earth.

I understood that we have roughly threescore and ten years on this orb of water and rock, and then we go back to where we came from – a vacation done kind of thing – but I thought this thing called life was pretty much ours, to do with as we would. I did not realise that it was an entity with its own agenda, a unique game with unfathomable rules.

Now, I realise that life is its own boss. Nobody tells it what to do. No one can argue with it, bribe it, or appease it.

IT JUST IS.

You can think you can debate with it using the same reasoning tools as the most advanced, logical thinkers, but life just laughs at you because life is not logical, so all of this goes over its head as it rolls remorselessly on its merry way.

Life is pure: it does not hold grudges, nor does it have sympathy for your cause. Because six million of you died in the latest holocaust and 20,000,000 in the previous one does not mean that life will say, "Ah...poor things – let me give them a free pass." It has no side to take since it has no heart to break, no sympathy or empathy to slow it down on its way to wherever it is going.

It cares not whether you are pretty, privileged, or poor, whether you have blue, brown, or hazel eyes. The fact that you have stolen more of your share of Gaia's resources does not mean that life will punish you. Life has no moral position to take on anything. It just would not notice if you are good or weak or strong. It has no future to plan. It is totally binary – it exists only in the now or the never.

Life has no memories to make it smile, no jokes to make it laugh, and no tears to shed over things that should or could have been.

It has no past, no commitments to slow it down, no debts to pay, no pay to collect, no parties to go to and no relationships that end reminding it of how lonely it truly is.

Do not sit there thinking that life is on your side, that it will forgive your mistakes, that you will somehow be allowed to get another chance.

Live life to the fullest. Make every second count. Be grateful that you are living in the now. Do not wish that your existence was in another time zone.

Be grateful for the relationships you have, the moral state in which you find yourself, the company you keep, the graciousness of the existence you have, and the relative peace of the time in which you find yourself.

Be grateful that life has brought you here to see, feel, and live this experience, but do not expect anything from life because it owes you nothing...

NOT EVEN YOUR NEXT BREATH!!

It would have been beneficial to realise all of this when I was 20-years-old.

The Nineteenth Thing I Wish I Knew

This, Too, Shall Pass

At 20. I never realised that I would fear death. I always thought that my courage would last me a lifetime and any anxiety or uncertainty would be short-lived. I thought this right up until I was 50. It was then that life presented the years of famine.

I call them the years of famine, but a better way to look at them is to call them years of learning. Until then, I did not know what real adversity was. Yes, I had been racially abused, burnt, had small accidents, and was hospitalised a few times, but most of these things only affected me temporarily, and I was always able to bounce back.

At 50, the real lessons came, and like the character, Job, from the Bible, I wondered, "Why me?" I found no answer to this question, but what I came to realise was that all things pass if you have the patience, will, and resilience to endure what you are going through in the present.

It will pass, the sun will shine again, your eyes will open once more, and your next breath will come...until it does not.

Just remind yourself that until you die, "This, too, will pass".

I use this as a mantra in moments of uncertainty. I did not really know what a mantra was at 20.

The Twentieth Thing I Wish I Knew

The World is made from Chaos with a Little Bit of Order Thrown in as an Afterthought

As I go around the seasons once more, getting older and listening more frequently to the news, more to occupy the empty space left by retirement than any real desire to learn anything new, it begins to feel as if we as a species, as a planet, as a universe exist in a state of pandemonium and everyone – no, every*thing* – is looking for the centre of the storm as it were, where it is peaceful and calm.

Everything wants its voice heard. Everything runs around, desperately trying all in its power to survive another minute, another day, another month, another decade, another billion years. All living things, from the tiny amoeba to the most massive galaxy, wants to be immortal.

The common cold wants to survive; it is fed up with shining its light for 48 hours before fading away. No, it wants to bob, weave, and hide in the corners of your lungs until it grows into pneumonia and matures into a chest infection – anything and everything to extend its life, even if it means ending yours.

Passion is born, matures into obsession, then ripens into madness. All of this because at some point along the journey, it decides, not that it wants to live, but that it does not want to die and will do anything to avoid that final curtain, even if it brings insanity.

Hatred is born out of fear and insecurity, and once it has been given the breath of life, it clings to it as a person holds onto a parachute on the way down. It will do anything to survive. In the end, the hatred develops a life and strategy for survival outside of the host in which it lives.

Nature does not want to die on its journey. It has given humanity a small window in which to exist and has allowed the intelligence it has given it to expand to the point where humans can extend their lives, which, with great serendipity, also extends nature's existence.

If I had known this at 20, I would have made sure that I did nothing to extend the life of negative things but promote the presence of good things. I would tell friends and colleagues not to tell anyone about their business until they were confident it would not be used negatively and through jealousy and fear, allow hatred to come to life.

I would urge people to seek out media outlets that reflect their culture and heritage and share good practices like discussing issues within the community so that we can grow and thrive together.

I would tell people to find the right balance between passion and obsession and walk away if they cannot control the crossover point between the two.

I would encourage people to see negative thoughts and actions as real-life forces trying to create chaos in their short lives and either convert them, change perceptions, or walk away.

People should live healthy and passionately but free from obsession and hate. Finding balance is the key. They should avoid chaos as long as they can and try to find the centre of the storm, where all is calm and tranquil.

Finally, do not be afraid of death when it comes, because it will come.

Finally, In Closing

A Homage to Desiderata ~ Stay Focused

I love the poem, *Desiderata*. I cannot be sure who wrote it, but it has been emblazoned on birthday cards, the back of books, seaside postcards, and a whole host of commercial memorabilia I have come across over the years.

I have gone for years not seeing or noticing it, and then it suddenly appears in the most unlikely of places.

It captures a pace, a way, a direction, and a moral code I wish I could use to plan the way I choose to live.

One day, I woke up and decided that I would rewrite it to make it even more relevant to me. It took me months to get it right, to find the right words that make it real to me. I have tried to live according to these ideas since writing them down. Sometimes, I fail miserably, but over the years, these words have become the guidelines I use to focus, direct, and plan the life I would like to lead, bearing in mind that life is not something you can tame.

I wish I had done it at 20, but then wisdom comes from time spent in pain, anguish, happiness, and joy. I might just have been too young to realise this at 20.

Stay Focused

Remember To:

Stay focused in the middle of the noise and bustle,
And remember the peace and tranquillity of silence.
While you are strong, there are occasions when being
Seen as being weak and fragile is the best line to take.
You don't have to wait until you are loved before you love.

Speak your truth quietly and clearly,
But listen. Listen to all information,
For sometimes, the wisest words
Are spoken by the biggest fools,
And everyone has an important story to tell.

Walk away from the rudeness of aggressive people
Once you have heard what they have to say.
Staying and returning their aggression
Makes you worse than they
For you know better.

Do not compare yourself with anyone else
For this will make you either vain or bitter,
For there will always be greater and
Lesser achievements than yours.
Take pride in what you do
And what you achieve.

Remember:
Dreams are reality, awaiting their time.
Stay focused on your dreams
For they are tomorrow's reality.
Pursue your career;
It is an important part of the baton
In the relay race of life.

Trust everyone until they prove
They cannot be trusted.
This may be painful now and then,
But in the long run of time,
You will find that people
Are virtuous...caring...loving...
Protective...heroic...giving...
And trustworthy.

Be yourself.
Evolve and grow.
Mature like wine,
But do not change.
See the world. Understand its strengths and weaknesses
But maintain and love your sense of self at all times.

Listen well to the words of the wise;
You will find that the years of life,
Seeing and observinwg, have made the elders
Arrive closer to the fundamental truths.

Some of them may appear as if they do not know,
But listen before dismissing them as fakes –
They may surprise you.

Keep your mind, your body, and your soul
Clean, healthy, and as pure as life will allow,
But do not become obsessed with this.
Remember: the ultimate enjoyment in life
Is when it all balances.

Do not seek loneliness for a friend,
But do not run away from the medicinal qualities
Of solitude.

Be gentle with yourself
In a disciplined way,
Forgetting not that you
Are a child of the universe
No greater than the atom, and
No less than the stars.
You were destined to be here.
Time and space is unfolding
Exactly as it was meant.

Be in harmony with your god –
Be it nature or Jehovah –
Whatever you decide it to be,
And remember:

In the confusion of pursuing your dreams,
Be at peace with yourself,
For with all its politics,
Pain...lies...deceit...wrongs...
And broken dreams,
It is still a beautiful world.

Stay Focused.

Acknowledgements

Would like to thank the Conscious Dreams Publishing team for all the outstanding effort and quality they brought to this project. They are all unbelievably, professional and talented. Cannot wait for my next book to work with you folks again.

A special thank you to my editor, Elise Abram, my typesetter, Oksana Kosovan, and making it all happen, Daniella Blechner, Book Journey Mentor and Publisher.

Thank you, team. Acknowledgement is given to Curtis Mayfield for some of the views expressed in the song *"We People Who Are Darker than Blue"* and to Bob Marley for some of the facts and opinions expressed in the song *"Redemption Song."*

Full acknowledgement is also given to the sources for the Trans Atlantic slave trade timeline. The main acknowledgements are given to Brycchan Carey's website, The George Beattie Project's website, and jicolerenaissance.wordpress.com/portugal-the-african-slave-trade

The poem *"Stay Focused"* was inspired by the work *"Desiderata"* and acknowledgement is given.

About the Author

Roy Merchant was born in Jamaica. He left there in 1961 to join his parents in England. He enlisted in the Royal Navy in 1965 and became a submariner, spending most of his submarine years in Singapore, Hong Kong and other parts of the Far East.

Having left the Navy in 1970, he retrained as an Electronics Engineer, then Technical Manager in a large television rental company in the 1970s.

In the mid-'80s, he moved into local government as a senior manager in a London local authority. Retiring in 2014, Roy took a new path and started a Health and Wellbeing company catering mainly for the African Caribbean community while dedicating more time to writing and performance poetry across London.

This book is his second, the first is entitled *Walking In The Shadows Of Death*.

Conscious Dreams

P U B L I S H I N G

Be the author of your own destiny

Find out about our authors, events, services
and how you too can get your book journey started.

Conscious Dreams Publishing

@DreamsConscious

@consciousdreamspublishing

Daniella Blechner

www.consciousdreamspublishing.com

info@consciousdreamspublishing.com

Let's connect

Lightning Source UK Ltd.
Milton Keynes UK
UKHW012201070720
366166UK00001B/49